Chakras

A Complete Guide to Chakra Healing

Jamie Parr

Table of Contents

Introduction

Chakras are phenomenal energy centers that exist within the metaphysical energy body. Discovering what your chakras are and how they work allows you to understand your own energy field, and then interact with it in a way that maximizes your quality of life in every way possible. Through a regular chakra balancing practice, you will discover a greater sense of harmony in your life and in yourself.

Aside from this sense of harmony, you will discover how other people's chakras work, too. This allows you to understand how imbalanced chakras manifest in others, which enables you to understand why others behave in ways that are not always compassionate, loving, or kind. Through this, you can actually develop a deeper sense of compassion for them, too, as you understand where their behaviors are coming from.

In this book, we will cover everything you need to know in order to confidently work with your own chakras, including working with their energy as well as balancing and maintaining them in a positive manner. You will discover how to create a deep sense of support and peace in your own life, as well as experience an improved quality of life overall.

Throughout the following chapters, we will discuss the 7 different chakras, what they are responsible for, how you can balance and unblock them, and what benefits you will gain from doing so.

Taking the time to work on your chakras and your spiritual health is an incredibly beneficial endeavor. While chakras are not yet a mainstream topic of conversation in the western world, in other cultures they have been talked about for thousands of years. As you will soon discover, the benefits of working with your chakras are innumerable, so congratulations on taking this first step towards working with these incredible energy centers!

Thank you for taking the time to read this book, I hope that you find it to be helpful!

Chapter 1: What Are the Chakras?

Chakras are meridian points within your body that represent different forms of energy, and each chakra relates to different experiences that you have in life. There are seven chakras located within your body, and over 100 located within your spiritual energy field. Each of these chakras is designed to support you in your physical, energetic, and spiritual experiences in life.

A History Lesson on Chakras

In the Western world, chakras have only been discussed for a few decades. However, chakras are actually an ancient concept that dates back to the year 1500! Chakras are mentioned in the earliest Hindu texts known as the Vedas, where records of early Hindu religious beliefs and practices were logged and kept for future generations.

The original writings about chakras defined them as being energy centers along the body that were used to represent different aspects of a person, such as the self, body, life, thoughts, emotions, and spirit. Each chakra located within your body is relevant to both your spiritual and physical life and can be used to enhance the quality of your life in one way or another. By working with the chakras, you are working with your "Prana" or life force energy, and you can actually manipulate and influence your life force energy through your chakras. The chakras are most commonly worked on through diet, yoga, meditation, and reiki. Other tools such as crystals, colors, and different forms of energy healing are also used to work with your chakras, though none of these reflect the original or traditional means for working with these energy centers.

The Purpose of your Chakras

Your chakras serve a multifaceted purpose in your life, bringing harmony between your physical body and your energy centers. They bridge the gap between your body and spirit, offering you a way to enhance your senses, increase your abilities in a variety of fields, and create a deeper understanding of life and the universe itself.

In modern society, a deep and meaningful connection to the spiritual self has largely been lost, as we have been taught to live without it. Rather than learning to trust your instinct, work with your energy, and ponder the ways to have a meaningful life, we are taught how to trust in the government, feed the system, and live widely disconnected from ourselves and our communities. Learning how to create space to engage in a more spiritual, energetic life means you grant yourself permission to tap into the entirety of what it means to be a human. In doing this, the level of understanding you will gain about yourself and your life will completely transform the quality of your life and what you gain from life itself. It truly is a holistic way of living.

If you add essential chakra self-care measures to an already wonderful self-care routine that includes a healthy diet, physical exercise, excellent sleep, mental and emotional wellness measures, and other such practices, you will experience a truly great quality of life. Even if you are already doing well in all other areas of your life, focusing your attention on your spiritual health will drastically improve your wellbeing.

What Chakras Actually are

Your chakras are said to be flat discs of energy that rotate clockwise over specific axis points on your body, within your metaphysical body. Your metaphysical body overlaps your physical body, often remaining anchored through meridians such as the chakras. All seven chakras are located along your spinal column, each having its own specific place where it remains. Some believe there is a single chakra located on the spine itself, while others believe you have one axis point in front of your spine and one behind it, and that an imbalanced chakra can be recognized as these two points being misaligned. Regardless of how you choose to visualize it, the general purpose of these chakras remains the same.

These rotating discs that exist along your chakra pillar each have their own color, symbol, and name. Certain people who have the ability to read and view auras can physically see chakras, allowing them to gain an understanding of a person's spiritual wellbeing. The seven chakras are represented by the colors of the rainbow: red, orange, yellow, green, blue, indigo, and violet. Each disc will glow brightly in its respective color and should move fluidly to indicate that it is in optimal health. A chakra that moves too slow or too fast, or that shines too bright or too dimly, is a chakra that is imbalanced and requires work to balance it once again. Imbalanced chakras bring about unwanted energies and often troubling manifestations of those energies, so it is important to always do your part to keep your chakras balanced.

Aside from how they look, each chakra has its own unique feeling. Each chakra has a distinct vibe that can easily be separated from the others in your chakra pillar. The easiest way to understand this concept would be to consider the three people that are closest to you in your life. Each of those three people has their own unique energy that is entirely different from anyone else, and that makes them, "them." The same goes for your chakras; each one carries distinct energy that helps them remain separate from the others, and which also makes them easily distinguishable from one another.

If a chakra is blocked or overactive, the energy associated with that chakra will be different. As you might imagine, chakras with blocked energy feel dull and seem to lack the vibrancy that they are supposed to have, while chakras with overactive energy will experience hyperactivity of their respective energy. For the most part, they feel overwhelming and may even manifest anxiety or similar feelings in the respective areas of their body.

As you learn more about each of your seven chakras, you will identify how they are supposed to feel and how to recognize when one has become blocked or overactive. This will allow you to intuitively understand the health of your chakras, and to know when they require attention and care.

Why you Need to Work with your Chakras

Since chakras themselves are not a part of our mainstream culture, you might wonder why they are so important. After all, if they were so important, wouldn't we already be talking about them, learning about them, and associating with them in our everyday lives, or as a part of our standard society? The answer is, no. Unfortunately, the western world largely lacks a fundamental understanding of spiritual energy and is void of commonplace information that could educate the collective about it. While this is slowly changing and people in the west are becoming more and more educated on spirituality, there is still a long way to go.

Working with your chakras will help you personally understand yourself in a far deeper way than any logical or practical information ever could.

As you begin to work with your chakras, you will likely discover a major change in your overall wellbeing. Everything from your mind, body, emotions, and spirit will be elevated through chakra work. This is not only due to a bridge in the gap between the physical and metaphysical, but due to the fact that this bridge brings with it a much deeper ability to interact with the life force energy of everything around you. You will begin to better understand and sense the energy emitted by both people and things, giving you a much clearer image of the world around you.

In your body, it is common to experience immense changes upon first working with the chakras. Your intuition about your wellbeing and ability to take care of yourself will improve as you are naturally called to eat healthier, move your body, and take good care of yourself. The improved flow of energy through your body will manifest in healthy functioning systems, an improved ability to heal, and a sort of glow that can only be achieved through working with yourself and your energy. Perhaps you have seen this in others who have a sort of inexplicable energy and glow that radiates from them.

Within your mind, working with your chakras will improve your understanding of the metaphysical world and will eliminate some of the questions you might have about the universe, spirit, and energy. Your deepened intuition will allow you to work in harmony with universal energies as you begin to flow with all that surrounds you. This can allow for incredible creativity in all types of art and expression. The validation and sense of inner peace that balanced chakras provide will transform your self-esteem and self-confidence.

Emotionally, working with your chakras deepens your level of self-care and creates space for you to understand the energy of your emotions and the meaning of them in a more complete way. Working on your chakras can itself be quite an intense emotional experience. Throughout this process you may have to let go of emotional pain from the past, acknowledge feelings that you have been repressing, and be honest with yourself about how you really feel deep down. While this may sound scary or intimidating, it ultimately is an incredibly rewarding and healing endeavor.

Spiritually, chakras facilitate an unparalleled relationship between your physical self and your energy. This relationship is most often described as experiencing a deeper sense of meaning from life itself. This relationship often makes a person's purpose in life become clear and obvious. This is because, once you tap into the entirety of who you are all the way down to a spiritual level, you begin to understand the total reality of what it means to be *you*.

Chapter 2: Benefits of Chakra Healing

Healing your chakras brings with it many different benefits that can improve your life in a variety of ways. Anytime you engage in a new practice, knowing and understanding that it can transform your life for the better is important. It means there is great value behind the energy you are putting in, and that your efforts are well worth it. The more you invest in your chakras, the more you will get out of them, and the better your life will become. In this chapter, we will discuss the many different areas of your life that may improve through working on your chakras.

Improved Overall Wellbeing

Improving your chakra health means that you are able to transmit valuable life force energy throughout your entire body. When all 7 chakras are clear and healthy, energy flows freely between them and throughout your body to where it is needed. This actually aids your body in staying in top shape physically, mentally, emotionally, and spiritually.

Greater Spiritual Fitness

Similar to physical health, spiritual fitness is important for your overall wellbeing. Beyond just basic self-care, investing into spiritual fitness will help you to reach a greater sense of enlightenment. When you have excellent spiritual fitness, you can even awaken your third eye and interact with the spiritual world around you through the various clair senses, with the most common being clairvoyance.

Removes Bad Energy from the Body

Balancing your chakras helps improve and stabilize your energy levels by removing bad energy from your space. When this negative energy is removed, you experience a greater ability to see the positive things in life. This provides an incredible boost to both mood, and motivation levels. Clean, balanced chakras promote relaxation and gentle energy that allows you to feel your best at all times. It is likely that you will feel better in ways that you did not even know were possible once you start activating and working with your chakras.

Increases Joy and Love in your Life

It is hard to know what you are missing out on in life until the blockages are removed, and you start to experience new things for the first time. When your chakras are unblocked, especially your sacral chakra which governs emotions, feelings like joy and love flood into your life because they are no longer restricted. You will likely feel an increase in spontaneity, positive energy, and a general sense of being emotionally uplifted as your chakras become unblocked.

Builds a Relationship Between you and your Inner Self

Each of us has a unique inner self that is different from the version of ourselves that we express to the world around us. Often, we refrain from having a relationship with our inner self because we are unaware of how vast and deep this version of ourselves truly is. Another common issue faced is a lack of confidence to express this inner self outwardly. When you take the time to work with your chakra energies, you are also working with aspects of your inner self, which enables you to tap into who you are in a deeper way. Over time, the voice that talks to you from within will become louder, clearer, and more familiar to you. You will begin to realize that it has been there all along, ready to help you through life and that it offers more than you ever could have possibly imagined. By tapping into this inner voice, you will discover who you really are and what you truly desire out of life. This clarity of self can provide an unmatched level of self-confidence, belief, and sense of purpose.

Transforms your Weaknesses to Strengths

Every one of us has weaknesses, and those weaknesses are made worse when we fail to acknowledge them or recognize them for what they truly are. When you take the time to acknowledge your weaknesses, you immediately eliminate some of their power because you are aware of what they are. Once you've acknowledged these weaknesses, you are then able to begin working on them. When you work with your chakras, your weaknesses will be illuminated. What you need to work on and overcome will become extremely clear, and this will allow you to face and overcome these shortcomings, ultimately turning them into strengths.

Improves your Financial Wisdom

Your chakras have impeccable strength, and among that strength exists natural financial wisdom that aids you in knowing how to make financial decisions, including spending in a smart way, and manifesting in a seemingly magical way. Those who routinely work with their chakras can *feel* the energy of money. They have a greater awareness of how to attract more into their lives, and how to use it in a way that keeps more coming in. As you continue to release blocks from your energy field and incorporate mantras and affirmations into your energy field in a deep and meaningful way, you begin to experience far greater wealth in your life. While financial pursuits don't excite everyone, healthy chakras allow for a level of manifestation that is hard to believe. This ability to manifest things into your life can be used for a variety of things, such as to find a partner, create the body you want, and of course, to achieve financial success.

Aids in your Successful Manifesting

You have more power in you than you can possibly dream of, and all of it is available to you right now. When you begin to clean and clear your chakras, you gain the ability to access your power and use it to manifest whatever you desire. This ability to manifest can be used to achieve practically anything, so long as your chakras are clear and your energy is focused intensely on what it is that you want.

Builds Your Intuition

Your intuition is housed within your energy body, which is precisely what your chakras govern. As you heal your chakras, you start to hear your inner self speak, providing you with divine knowledge and guidance. Whether it is guidance offered by your higher self, your spirit guides, your guardian angels, the universe, or any divine entity, it can all be heard and felt through your intuition. You can also begin to awaken and activate your third eye chakra and psychic abilities once you are in touch with your chakras and the energy within them.

Increases Healthy Emotional Release

Emotions are all a form of energy, and when you work with energy, you discover how to use it and allow it to flow in a more meaningful manner. As you activate and work with your chakras, you may begin to experience an increase in your healthy emotional releases. Most people, particularly in Western society, repress their emotions, and hide their true feelings. This all results in an unhealthy build-up of energy. The more you work with your chakras, the healthier your emotional expressions will become. You will gain a better understanding of the emotions you are feeling, and instead of bottling them up inside, you will be able to release them in a natural and healthy way. Your emotions will no longer be passive experiences, but rather, active opportunities to improve the quality of your life.

Chapter 3: Root Chakra

Your root chakra is the first of your seven primary physical chakras. Before working with any of your higher chakras, you need to balance your root chakra to provide yourself with a solid foundation. As a way to create that solid foundation, the root chakra is associated with survival and the basics of wellbeing on a physical level.

Root Chakra Overview

The *Muladhara*, or your root chakra, is located at the base of your tailbone and glows a vibrant red color when it is active and balanced. This chakra is associated with your primordial brain or the instinctive parts of who you are. Every primal urge you have, from eating and sleeping to competing and surviving, all stem from your root chakra.

Correspondences and Connections

Your root chakra, as with all chakras, corresponds with different herbs, crystals, and body parts. There are also symbols, sounds, and other correspondences that correlate to each chakra, but as you are just starting out, it is best to keep it simple.

The root chakra responds best to herbs like angelica, cayenne, cinnamon, ginger, clove, raspberry leaf, and turmeric. Each of these can be blended into foods or drinks, offering you a way to nourish your root chakra from the inside out. If you like working with essential oils, you can expand into herbs and resins such as frankincense, myrrh, or cedar. Each of these can be diffused, diluted, used to anoint your body, or incorporated into room sprays as a way to elevate the health of your root chakra.

Crystals like black tourmaline, green jasper, garnet, rhodochrosite, rose quartz, and ruby are all wonderful for your root chakra. You can use these crystals by carrying them with you, wearing them, placing them near the base of your spine when you are meditating, or decorating your home with them as a way to bring forth their powerful, healing energies.

Physically, your root chakra correlates to your tailbone, anus, large intestine, adrenal glands, legs, feet, and back. Your bones are also governed by your root chakra, as they represent the solid physical connection that your body has to the earth beneath you. Your teeth are included in the bones that are governed by your root chakra.

Characteristics and Energetic "Personality"

The root chakra heavily impacts your "survival" personality. Each of us has a unique "survivor mode" we can click into as needed, which allows us to persevere through any challenge we may face. You may find yourself mentally and emotionally shutting down as you focus on the physical aspects of survival, possibly even finding yourself narrowing in on your instinctive abilities and discovering how you can maneuver through anything you are faced with. Some people even report having deep urges to hunt, gather, and resort to a more primal way of life when their root chakra is particularly active because they are in such deep connection with their primal state.

Beyond your state of survival, your root chakra holds your identity in question. Part of its "personality" is to wonder who you are, where you came from, and how you fit into the world around you, as belonging to your community plays a large role in your survival. Anytime you question your identity, you are feeling the energy of your root chakra rise up and course through you, as it seeks ways to protect you.

Influence on your Health

When the root chakra is imbalanced, it can play a major role in the health of your bones, as well as your lower organs and hormones. People who experience either a blocked or overactive root chakra can experience anything from osteoporosis to pain in the lower back, legs, and feet. Hormonal issues, especially relating to digestion, can become problematic when your root chakra is imbalanced, as well. You might experience strained or excessive bowel movements, as well as cramping and discomfort in your lower intestines. If stress is imminent, you might also experience problems with your teeth, either due to increased stomach acid breaking them down, or grinding your teeth as a result of stress.

Lessons of the Root Chakra

The root chakra teaches you the importance of recognizing that you are a capable, resilient individual who has everything you need to survive. It allows you to break free from emotional bondage and elevate your personal strength by taking your wellbeing into your own hands and protecting yourself and your sense of identity. As you do this, your bravery and courage will grow, and you will be able to feel better on your own. This chakra also helps you to understand your unique role in your community and life, and then use that as an opportunity to deepen your connection to those around you. Healing any trauma you may have faced in childhood, such as neglect or abandonment, can also help balance your root chakra.

Symptoms of a Blocked Root Chakra

If your root chakra is blocked, tension will rise through your tailbone and build up in your lower body, creating dull aches and feelings of fullness in your trunk, legs, and feet. You may also experience co-dependency, fear of abandonment, a lack of focus, anxiety, fearfulness, guilt, depression, and resentment as a result of your root chakra being imbalanced. Physical diagnoses like hypertension, colitis, sciatica, impotence, prostate issues, eating disorders, irritable bowel syndrome, and unexplained pain in the trunk, legs, and feet are all an indication that your root chakra has become imbalanced. It is important that you take practical physical healing measures in addition to spiritual healing measures in order to completely recover. This ensures that your physical symptoms are cared for whilst the root cause is simultaneously dealt with.

Symptoms of an Overactive Root Chakra

Overactive root chakras lead to restlessness or hyperactivity, as well as feelings of rage and aggression. While you might not act on these symptoms, you may find yourself feeling ready to defend yourself in a seemingly excessive manner. High blood pressure is a common diagnosis for those with an overactive root chakra, too. Overactive root chakras are often caused by a threat to your survival. For example, if you were abandoned as a child, if you live in poverty, or if you experienced a near-death experience, you may have developed an overactive root chakra as a result. The more overactive your chakra is, the more anxious, controlling, and aggressive you are likely to become.

Routine for a Balanced Root Chakra

Balancing your root chakra starts by taking practical measures such as eating a proper diet, securing your finances, and ensuring that you have a safe and secure roof over your head. This way, you are able to guarantee your chances of survival and take some pressure off of yourself so you can feel safer in your environment.

In addition to practical measures, you can begin to wear root chakra jewelry or carry a crystal with you that is designed to help you support your root chakra. Garnet is a particularly powerful one, as it helps you keep your root chakra as grounded, protected, and balanced as possible.

If your root chakra is overactive, increase your intake of earthy foods and herbs, eating things like beetroots, potatoes, and garlic on a more regular basis. If your root chakra is blocked, eat things that are spicy to fire up this chakra and get your energy flowing.

Meditating on your root chakra can help you balance it, as well. Daily meditations focused on your root chakra can help you bring it back into balance if you find it has become imbalanced. If your root chakra is already in a state of balance, you can do the full chakra healing meditation from Chapter 10 as a way to keep your root chakra, as well as all of your other chakras, balanced.

The meditation you can use specifically for your root chakra is best done by sitting with your legs crossed, and your tailbone pressed down toward the earth. Anoint yourself with frankincense, myrrh, or cedar essential oils, and keep a piece of garnet in your hand. Cup your hands low, next to your root chakra, so the crystal is nice and close. Then, close your eyes and enter a meditative state by following a simple, slow breathing pattern. Once you begin to feel relaxed, visualize your root chakra and the energy it contains. If it is overactive, visualize its movements slowing down, and it emitting an even, balanced light. If it is blocked, visualize its movements speeding up and its color brightening as you bring it back into a state of action. Once you feel your chakra is balanced, visualize a "root" growing out of your root chakra and into the ground below you, connecting you to the earth. This connection acts as a constant source of balancing energy for your root chakra. Visualize and feel the powerful energy coming from the earth and into your root chakra, flowing freely.

Repeat this meditation on a regular basis, while also taking other measures such as changing your diet and using crystals. In a short period of time, you will notice your root chakra becoming balanced and your sense of safety and wellbeing improving.

Chapter 4: Sacral Chakra

Your sacral chakra is your second chakra, located just above your root chakra. This chakra is rooted in sensual energy and is deeply connected to your physical senses. It is ideal to work on your sacral chakra intentionally and privately, while also being protective over who you allow into this intimate energy space. This way, you can keep your sacral chakra safe, well-balanced, and at peace.

Sacral Chakra Overview

Your *Svadhisthana,* or sacral chakra, is located slightly below your belly button. For females, it is directly associated with the sexual organs of your ovaries, uterus, and vagina. The sacral chakra is represented by a bright orange color, representing your passion and fire for life, as well as your drive to create. Your sacral chakra deeply corresponds to a sense of community, primarily around building and supporting community, rather than belonging to a community or relying on your community for survival. In order to properly balance your sacral chakra, you will first require a balanced root chakra, as this ensures you have a solid foundation to balance your sacral chakra on.

Correspondences and Connections

All of the things that correspond with your sacral chakra also correspond with your senses and your sensual energy. Herbs such as cinnamon, cardamom, clove, orange peel, and ginger are all great for your sacral chakra. Raspberry leaf is also excellent. Essential oils like rose, ylang ylang, and orange are also wonderful for your sacral chakra, as well as any other citrusy oils.

Crystals like bloodstone, moonstone, hematite, rhodochrosite, orange calcite, and garnet are all excellent for your sacral chakra. You can carry them in your pocket as this keeps them close to your sacral chakra. However, they can also be worn as jewelry or kept in your vicinity as a way to send their energy your way.

Physically, your sacral chakra corresponds with feminine reproductive organs, as well as the bladder, kidneys, large intestine, and hips. If you have a menstrual cycle, the entire cycle is also governed by your sacral chakra, including all of the hormones and organs responsible for contributing to your cycle.

Characteristics and Energetic "Personality"

Creativity, intimacy, and sexuality are the three primary energies that relate to your sacral chakra. When you partake in hobbies, nurture relationships, or deepen your sense of connection to anyone or anything around you, you are working with your sacral chakra. Every streak of creativity or inspiration you experience, either through self-expression, personal style, or art that you create, is rooted in your sacral chakra. While your sacral chakra and sexuality are closely linked, it is important to understand that this means your chakra governs your sexual identity and not just the act of sex itself. In fact, many monks and people from various cultures and faiths are intentionally celibate because they believe this increases the power of their sacral chakra by keeping it pure and within the body.

Influence on Your Health

Your sacral chakra is most likely to affect your reproductive health, especially if you are a female. Your fertility, the quality of your menstrual cycle, and all of your sexual hormones are impacted by your sacral chakra. If your sacral chakra is blocked, imbalances in your sexual or reproductive hormones may occur. Females may experience painful menstruation or a lack of menses, reduced fertility, cysts, dryness, or other problems relating to their sexual hormones. Men may experience erectile dysfunction, loss of fertility, and issues relating to imbalances in their hormones, too.

Lessons of the Sacral Chakra

Your sacral chakra encourages you to recognize yourself as a sensual, talented being with a deep need for intimate connections with yourself, those around you, and the universe as a whole. Sharing healthy, intimate relationships with people in different ways, depending on the role they play in your life, is a wonderful way to discover the power of this chakra.

Symptoms of a Blocked Sacral Chakra

If you have a blocked sacral chakra, you will experience a lack of creativity, limited inspiration, and even a reduced sexual appetite. Some people with a blocked sacral chakra also feel a sense of confusion or isolation as they struggle to intimately and emotionally connect with others. You may also feel as though you are unloved, unimportant, or unaccepted. Often, those with a blocked sacral chakra will commit acts of self-sabotage that lead to an inability to fulfill their desires. You may also experience anxiety or other emotional troubles related to your inability to express your creativity or your sexuality.

Symptoms of an Overactive Sacral Chakra

If your chakra is overactive, you may experience addictions, especially addiction to sex or other highly sensual activities. You may even engage in dangerous thrill-seeking behaviors in an effort to fulfill your constant sensual cravings and desires. It can also be easy to misinterpret the relationships in your life, having unrealistic or inappropriate expectations for the level of intimacy that you should be experiencing with others. You may also find yourself burning bridges as soon as relationships are no longer fulfilling to you. This typically occurs when you find yourself experiencing an energetic void within, and you may blame others in your life for that void's existence.

Routine for a Balanced Sacral Chakra

If your sacral chakra is already balanced, the meditation in Chapter 10 will be plenty to keep it balanced on a day to day basis. If your sacral chakra is not already balanced, though, there are many things you can do to help balance your sacral chakra once more.

If your sacral chakra is blocked *or* overactive, drinking teas made of orange or citrusy blends can help bring your chakra into a more balanced state. Dancing, drawing, painting, and other art forms are also wonderful for balancing your sacral chakra, as they encourage you to work with the sensual energies of your chakra. If your chakra is overactive, the art you create may be more hectic as it allows you to release the excess energies you have been carrying. If your chakra is blocked, your art may be more timid, but it *will* help you unlock and activate your energies as you continue to express yourself through your art.

Since the sacral chakra plays such a huge role in your emotions, it is important to learn how to balance your emotions, too. Practical skills such as learning to emotionally relate to others and build healthy intimate relationships in your life is a great way to balance your sacral chakra. You can do this either on your own, working toward having a healthy mindset around your relationships, or you can work with a therapist if you find you have difficulty doing this on your own.

When meditating to balance your sacral chakra, it is ideal to lay down so you can gently rest both of your hands over your lower abdomen, where your sacral chakra is located. You may wish to hold a piece of orange calcite, moonstone, bloodstone, or other crystal against your sacral chakra to assist with balancing your energies. Anointing yourself with a corresponding essential oil is also a great way to help balance your sacral chakra. Once you are ready, take several deep, calming breaths to help yourself enter a relaxing, meditative state. Once you are relaxed, you can start focusing on your sacral chakra. Draw your attention down to your sacral chakra and become aware of its color and movement, taking note of how it is functioning. If it is moving slowly or appears dull in color, breathe energy into it, encouraging it to become more vibrant and energized. Visualize it spinning more consistently and glowing more vibrantly until you have a bright, healthy chakra. Conversely, if your chakra is moving so quickly that it causes anxiety or is glowing so bright that it's hard to tell what color it truly is; you can adjust this by breathing calming energy into it. Encourage it to slow down and glow brightly but not excessively. Control your breathing and visualize energy flowing freely through your sacral chakra. When you feel more at peace with your sacral chakra, you can end your meditation. You should repeat this regularly until you feel as though your sacral chakra is balanced and healthy on a consistent basis.

Chapter 5: Solar Plexus Chakra

Your solar plexus chakra is the third of the seven chakras. This chakra brings forth a mighty power that often scares people when they first interact with it, especially if they are faced with an overactive chakra, or the need to activate one that has been imbalanced. The power of your solar plexus chakra is enormous and impressive. Learning to work with your solar plexus chakra will drastically improve your wellbeing, increase your sense of personal power, and create space for you to enjoy a strong, energetic pillar within yourself. By balancing it correctly, you can safely work on higher energies within yourself, such as your third eye chakra.

Solar Plexus Chakra Overview

Your *Manipura,* or solar plexus chakra, is located directly over your solar plexus, which is about three finger widths below the center of your rib cage, or 3-4 inches above your belly button. This chakra is represented by the color yellow, and it is said to be the seat of your soul as it links your spiritual self with your physical self, serving as the connection between your lower and higher chakras.

Correspondences and Connections

Your solar plexus chakra is heavily associated with your digestive system and your digestive hormones and enzymes. It is important that you nurture it with a healthy diet, proper herbs, and plenty of water. Herbs like milk thistle, calendula, dandelion, ginger, turmeric, chamomile, and lemon balm are all great for your solar plexus chakra. These can be used in dishes you cook, or in teas you drink, depending on how you prefer to consume them. You can also use essential oils like geranium, grapefruit, or ginger, all of which are wonderful for your solar plexus chakra.

Crystals like carnelian, aventurine, citrine, gold, pyrite, yellow calcite, tiger's eye, and topaz are all excellent for working with your solar plexus chakra. Wearing these on long necklaces, as rings, or placing them over your solar plexus chakra while you meditate are the most powerful ways to infuse these energies into your solar plexus chakra.

The specific body parts that correspond with your solar plexus chakra include your gallbladder, spleen, stomach, and liver. Your skin, and especially how you physically see yourself, are also associated with your solar plexus chakra. The more you take care of your digestive system, your metabolism, and your skin, the healthier your solar plexus chakra will be.

Characteristics and Energetic "Personality"

Your solar plexus chakra carries the personality of your ego and your personal power. The energy relates to that of the sun, creating a fiery and powerful energy, which makes it feel as though you are tapping into the most powerful aspects of who you are. The more you balance your solar plexus chakra, the more empowered you will feel. This chakra brings forth great inner strength and personal connection, creating a sense of independence and, at times, arrogance as you tend to care only about yourself and your own wellbeing when working with this chakra.

Your intuitive voice is located within your solar plexus chakra, so the more you tap into this chakra, the louder your "gut feeling" will become. This chakra is important to your personal growth, with the growth you experience here being empowering, enjoyable, and sometimes challenging. As you remain plugged into your solar plexus chakra, you also remain plugged into a constant stream of power that drives you to become the best version of yourself possible. Personal development, power, and ego are the key aspects for this chakra.

Influence on Your Health

Since your solar plexus chakra largely governs your metabolism and digestive system, you can likely guess that your solar plexus chakra is responsible for your digestive health. Eating healthy probiotics, maintaining a proper diet, and encouraging excellent gut health is a great way to keep your solar plexus chakra healthy. You can also balance your solar plexus chakra through working on your mental health, as your experiences of self-confidence and self-esteem are largely driven through this chakra. The more you are able to master your mental health and your personal power, the stronger this chakra will become.

Lessons of the Solar Plexus Chakra

The solar plexus chakra seeks to teach you that you are a powerful, independent, and eternal being. It wants you to understand that you can rely on yourself, trust in your ability to remain resilient through anything you are faced with, and experience peace within yourself. You are deserving and worthy of love, and you are capable of experiencing all of the wonderful things in life, and this chakra wants to help you fulfill that. When you are willing to make space for yourself and commit to thriving in life, your solar plexus chakra thrives, too. Be brave, courageous, and embrace life in as many ways as you possibly can. The more you own and respect your personal power, the stronger you will become! Don't forget to stay humble, though. True power is quiet in nature...

Symptoms of a Blocked Solar Plexus Chakra

If your solar plexus chakra is blocked, you might experience an identity crisis combined with a lack of confidence and self-esteem. You may not love or accept yourself and might struggle to assert yourself or your boundaries around others. It may seem far too easy for you to allow others to walk all over you and disrespect you. It can seem challenging to admit that you are not okay with how others are behaving, and confrontation can seem daunting beyond belief. Skin conditions like pimples, blackheads, and other breakouts can also occur as a result of a blocked solar plexus chakra.

Symptoms of an Overactive Solar Plexus Chakra

An overactive solar plexus chakra is often identified in individuals who are egotistical, arrogant, and who are too proud to receive guidance from anyone else. If you feel untouchable, like you are somehow better than everyone else, or like you have so much self-confidence you never question yourself, it is likely that you have an overactive solar plexus chakra. When this chakra is overactive, it can lead to major insecurities, as well as a shield around you that is seemingly impenetrable. This shield may sound like a good thing, but the reality is that the shield often becomes so strong that people see you as being bullheaded and have a hard time getting through to you or relating to you in any way, whatsoever. Often, this drives people away, or can lead to you engaging in toxic relationships with others.

Routine for a Balanced Solar Plexus Chakra

If your solar plexus chakra is already balanced, a total chakra healing is plenty to help keep your chakra balanced on a day to day basis. You can find a simple routine in Chapter 10. Otherwise, you need to take specific action to balance your solar plexus chakra.

First and foremost, you need to focus on your gut health. Incorporate foods into your diet that are rich with probiotics and other good bacteria for your gut. Drink plenty of water, and consume foods that are yellow in color, such as lemon, spaghetti squash, or mangoes. Turmeric tea is excellent for the health of your solar plexus chakra, too.

Wear necklaces or carry the crystal yellow citrine, as this is known for gently yet powerfully balancing your solar plexus chakra. Tiger's eye can also be used to help protect this chakra, as it protects against both low and excessive energies building up in this chakra.

To meditate on healing this chakra, relax in a seated position. If you can, do this outside on the grass or the soil, as the direct connection to the earth will be helpful with balancing this chakra. When you are ready, begin engaging in deep belly breaths, slowly calming yourself into a meditative state. If your solar plexus chakra is underactive or blocked, breathe activating energies into it. Draw energy up through the earth into your solar plexus chakra, and visualize this energy empowering your chakra to awaken and activate. If your solar plexus chakra is overactive, visualize the excess energy being removed through your root chakra as it "drains" back into the earth beneath you. Feel the energy flowing between the earth and your body, visualizing it moving up through your root chakra, into your sacral chakra, and then finally into the solar plexus chakra. Picture this healing energy flowing up and into your solar plexus chakra with every inhale, and any negative energy being expelled out of your body as you exhale. When you feel sufficiently balanced, you may end your meditation. Repeat it as often as you need to in order to thoroughly balance your solar plexus chakra.

Remember to check in with this chakra often and take note of how it feels, as this is an incredible powerful energy center. Too much energy in this chakra may at first feel normal, but can quickly escalate to egotism, so be careful.

Chapter 6: Heart Chakra

Your heart chakra is the fourth of your seven chakras on your physical chakra pillar. It represents your emotions in a more primal and less sensual way than the sacral chakra. As a collective, we are all working toward a major heart chakra healing, as everyone is discovering how to experience meaningful compassion toward themselves and others. Many are grieving, hurting, and generally feeling drained by our society and the current structure of our modern world. Learning how to heal your own heart chakra and live with a balanced heart chakra will drastically support you in maintaining a healthy energy field, while also supporting the rest of the world in maintaining one, too. As you work with your heart chakra, you will find yourself navigating and expressing your emotions in a far healthier manner, making it easier for you to enjoy the energy of your emotions as a whole.

Heart Chakra Overview

Your *Anahata,* or heart chakra, is located directly over your physical heart and is represented by the color green. Some people also associate pink with the chakra, as pink is a gentle and loving color that invokes peaceful emotions and healing. Your heart chakra is responsible for your ability to love unconditionally, navigate your emotions peacefully, and heal any emotional trauma you have ever experienced. When you keep your heart chakra balanced, you remain open to enjoying loving and positive emotional experiences. You also will become more resilient when faced with troubling or uncomfortable emotional experiences.

Correspondences and Connections

Your heart chakra governs your physical heart, as well as your circulatory system. Herbs that promote heart health, or the health of your circulatory system, are beneficial for your heart chakra. This includes herbs like lavender, rose, white peony, hawthorn, lemon balm, motherwort, yarrow, and vervain. As with any herbs, always check with your doctor to ensure they do not contraindicate any medications you may be taking or any symptoms you may be having. If you wish to use essential oils, use lavender, jasmine, or rose for your heart chakra.

Crystals like chrysocolla, chrysoprase, covellite, emerald, jadeite, rhodochrosite, and aventurine are all great for your heart chakra. Rose quartz, tourmaline, amazonite, kunzite, mango calcite, and smoky quartz are also great for helping to heal any emotional traumas you may be carrying with you. Wear your crystals on a necklace or place them over your heart chakra during meditation to get the most out of them.

Your heart chakra governs your heart and circulatory system, as well as your tears and your emotions. Anything you can do to support these systems within your body, such as exercising and eating to support your heart health, will help your heart chakra, too.

Characteristics and Energetic "Personality"

Your heart longs to love everything unconditionally, including yourself. It is a sensitive, vulnerable chakra to work with, so you may find yourself experiencing massive amounts of grief and pain when you first start. However, you will begin to experience far more positive emotions as you continue working with your heart chakra and tapping into the feelings of unconditional love.

Your heart chakra will allow you to express unconditional love for yourself and others during times when it is easy to love, as well as during times when it is not. For example, when you find yourself engaging in acts of self-sabotage rooted in emotions of fear, guilt, or shame, your heart chakra will long to love you unconditionally through it. This unconditional love will allow you to break free from the cycle of self-sabotage, and to shift your energy towards self-love.

Working with your heart chakra will also allow you to experience unconditional love for others, no matter who they are or what they have done. You learn to see the human in everyone and respect the fact that everyone goes through tough times, with many having experiences you cannot possibly fathom. As you learn to accept everyone for their own pains and traumas and recognize that this is a natural part of life, you start to find yourself tapping into the true value of the heart chakra.

Influence on your Health

With its effect on your heart, blood, and circulatory system, the heart chakra plays a massive role in your overall health. Heart disease or heart conditions, blood issues, and problems with your circulatory system all indicate that something is wrong with your heart chakra. For example, high blood pressure, heart attack, or an enlarged heart all indicate that you have an overactive heart chakra. Alternatively, low blood pressure, poor circulation, and cardiac arrest all indicate there is a blockage in your heart chakra. Releasing emotions can help physically move out any energy blockages, which may be leading to these physical blockages, effectively improving your overall health.

Lessons of the Heart Chakra

The heart chakra wants to teach you to love yourself, others, and everything in general. It wants you to recognize that every minute detail of this universe was put in place just for you, and that there are many wonderful blessings scattered throughout your life. As you learn to surrender and accept the emotional experiences of life, you realize that emotions are not as burdensome as you may have originally thought and that they actually hold great value. While emotions like anger and sadness may be more difficult to endure, there are also wonderful emotions like gratitude and happiness.

When your heart chakra is activated and awakened, it teaches you to release your bondages to feelings like anger, betrayal, hurt, jealousy, or injustice. You will continue to experience these challenging emotions, but you will no longer remain obsessed with them or needlessly attached to them, meaning they will naturally fade away over time. You will learn to acknowledge them, understand why you are experiencing them, and then move on. The only time emotions remain permanent is when you allow yourself to stay deeply attached to them. All emotions were meant to be temporary, and when you release your attachments to them, they remain temporary, and you experience them for what they truly are. That experience in and of itself is beautiful.

Symptoms of a Blocked Heart Chakra

If your heart chakra is blocked, you are likely to notice an inability to express your emotions, or even to feel them clearly. You may feel emotionally numb, or as though you have a lack of emotions to express overall. It may seem like you cannot connect to anyone or anything, because your ability to experience the emotions relating to those connections are blocked, and you cannot find it within yourself to summon them. Physically, you might suffer symptoms like blocked arteries, poor circulation, or low blood pressure as a result on a blocked heart chakra.

Symptoms of an Overactive Heart Chakra

If your heart chakra is overactive, you will experience things like excessive emotional responses to triggers, or inappropriate emotional attachments to people and things around you. A great example would be people who hoard objects that remind them of past memories, as they are holding unhealthy attachments and obsessions to the emotions linked to those memories. Other symptoms include overreacting to small inconveniences, taking other's emotions on as their own, or being so emotional that you let other people take advantage of you because you are afraid of letting anyone down. You may experience high blood pressure, an enlarged heart, or tachycardia as a response to your overactive heart chakra, as well.

Routine for a Balanced Heart Chakra

If your heart chakra is already balanced, the complete chakra balancing meditation from Chapter 10 will be plenty to help you maintain that balance. Otherwise, you can use the following routine to help you maintain a balanced chakra. Adjust your approach depending on whether you have a blocked or overactive chakra.

Eating foods like kiwi, cucumber, watermelon, and leafy greens is an excellent way to support your heart health. You can also drink teas that are made to promote heart health, such as green tea, oolong, or white tea, which are all great for you. You can also dab heart activating essential oil blends over your heart chakra, which will help you maintain a balanced chakra. On top of this, engaging in some cardiovascular exercise on a regular basis, be it playing a sport, running, or simply going for walks is a great way to promote heart health. Remember, it is important to take a holistic approach to health. It is not enough to just meditate to maintain the health of our chakras, we must also exercise, eat well, and get plenty of rest.

Working through your emotions on an ongoing basis by discussing them, expressing them in a healthy manner, or talking to a therapist is a great way to maintain your heart chakra's health, too. You can also use meditation, which is a wonderful way to release emotions while also breathing relaxing energy into your heart chakra.

As you meditate, lay down so your heart chakra can be close to the earth below you. Place a crystal over your heart chakra, preferably rose quartz unless you specifically feel drawn to one of the other crystals associated to the heart chakra. Start breathing deeply, allowing yourself to fall into a state of relaxation. If your heart chakra is blocked, you can visualize energy moving up through the earth to support your heart chakra and gently elevate it into a state of balance. See it moving in a steady clockwise motion and glowing vibrant green. If your heart chakra is overactive, visualize the excess energy melting into the earth below you as it is moved away from your heart chakra. Visualize your chakra gently slowing down and glowing a more steady, balanced color of green. Be patient with yourself if any emotions arise, giving yourself the space to express them as needed. When working with the heart chakra, some people feel the need to have an emotional release through crying, laughing, or yelling. Don't feel embarrassed or confused if you feel these urges, and instead, simply give in and allow yourself to release those excess emotions. This can be a very healing experience. When you feel as though your heart chakra is balanced, allow yourself to awaken back to the room around you. Repeat this meditation as often as is needed, until your heart chakra feels deeply balanced.

Chapter 7: Throat Chakra

Your throat chakra is the fifth of your seven physical chakras. This chakra governs your ability to communicate, share your thoughts, and invoke change in the world around you. Your throat chakra is more powerful than you might think, despite the fact that it is often stated as being "only" associated with your ability to communicate. Through it, you can provide and gain great amounts of value that are inaccessible through any other chakra or means. Keeping this chakra balanced is essential if you wish to communicate and interact with others effectively.

Throat Chakra Overview

Your *Vishuddha,* or throat chakra, is located in the hollow of your throat. It is represented by the color blue and is engaged anytime you express your thoughts or communicate with others. You can impact change through this chakra, either in your own life, in the lives of others, or in the world as a whole. This chakra can carry lasting consequences, which is why it is essential to balance this chakra and be careful to avoid expressing yourself when it is imbalanced, as doing so can lead to expressing yourself in ways you did not intend to. Your throat chakra has the power to connect you or separate you from those around you, so you must be intentional in how you activate it.

Correspondences and Connections

Your throat chakra is one of the most powerful tools you have as a human. You can nourish it using herbs like chamomile, sage, slippery elm, marshmallow, pleurisy root, thyme, or stillingia. Flowers like calendula, cosmos, heather, larch, scarlet monkeyflower, snapdragon, and trumpet vine also correspond with the throat chakra. If you use essential oils, use oils like basil, chamomile, or cypress.

If you wish to use crystals with your throat chakra, use those with vibrant hues of blue. Azurite, blue lace agate, lapis lazuli, and sapphire are all great for working with your throat chakra. Wear them on a necklace, or as earrings, to keep them close to the throat chakra.

Physically, your throat chakra corresponds with your mouth, throat, nose, and ears. Your lips, gums, teeth, tongue, tonsils, uvula, and esophagus are also associated with your throat chakra.

Characteristics and Energetic "Personality"

Your throat chakra is expressed through communication, offering you the ability to uplift, inspire, and motivate change, or the ability to provoke fear, anger, and hate. When your throat chakra is balanced, you find yourself experiencing the ability to easily communicate your thoughts, needs, and feelings with others. You can support others in becoming their best selves, while also motivating yourself to become your best self, too. Sometimes, you can inspire the best in yourself and others by speaking words of inspiration, while other times, the best way to support others is through staying quiet or keeping to yourself. When you have a balanced throat chakra, you will know exactly when to speak up, and when to stay quiet.

Influence on Your Health

Your throat chakra can have a major impact on virtually every area of health within your life. Physical, mental, and emotional health factors can all be affected by your throat chakra. When your throat chakra is in good health, it feels easy to speak as you have no emotional or mental hang ups, and your throat and mouth feel good. When it is blocked or overactive, you may have emotional or mental hang ups preventing you from sharing, or you may feel as though there is a lump in your throat. Some people even develop throat infections when they begin awakening their throat chakra, or if they allow it to remain dormant for too long, because of how damaged the energy in this area can become. Earaches, damage to the nostrils, and damage to the esophagus can also be caused by an imbalanced throat chakra.

Lessons of the Throat Chakra

Your throat chakra wants to show you how to create change, inspire others, and motivate those around you by teaching you how to communicate clearly, confidently, compassionately, and assertively. Forgiveness is a major lesson of the throat chakra, as it wants to teach you how to communicate and express forgiveness for yourself and others. In order to achieve this, your throat chakra first brings the awareness of forgiveness to your mind. Then, your heart chakra processes the forgiveness, and finally, your throat chakra communicates it.

Confessions, communication, and the ability to assert yourself all come from your throat chakra. Anytime you verbally "birth" a new idea to those around you, assert your needs, or confess your inner truth, you are working with your throat chakra. The more you work with it, the easier it will be for you to remain honest, and clearly assert yourself and express your thoughts and feelings.

Symptoms of a Blocked Throat Chakra

If your throat chakra is blocked, you may feel as though you have a lump in your throat, or like something is preventing you from speaking. You may feel as though something is physically pushing you back or silencing you every time you try to talk, even though you might not be able to describe what, specifically, is blocking you. Throat infections, swollen tonsils, and earaches that give a feeling of fullness also indicate that you have a blocked throat chakra. Emotionally and mentally, you might start blocking yourself off from others, holding back your opinions, or silencing yourself in an effort to maintain the peace in various situations. When this happens, you can feel confident that you have a blocked throat chakra, and that the blockages will likely get worse based on your continued actions.

Symptoms of an Overactive Throat Chakra

If you have an overactive throat chakra, it may seem like you are always talking, possibly even overstepping boundaries with the things you say. You might suffer from laryngitis, a loss of your voice, or a sore throat caused by excessive communication. If you speak harshly, say things you regret, speak without thinking, or fail to truly listen to what others are saying, you likely have a blocked throat chakra. All of these disturbances can lead to arguments, heated debates, or even burnt bridges as you focus more on being right and less on being kind and living in harmony with those around you.

Routine for a Balanced Throat Chakra

If your throat chakra is already balanced, it can be incorporated as the fifth chakra you focus on when you do your full chakra balancing meditation from Chapter 10. If your throat chakra is imbalanced, though, you will need to take necessary action to unblock your underactive, or relax your overactive, throat chakra.

Eating foods like blueberries, eggplants, blackberries, and haskap berries are all excellent for nurturing your throat chakra. You can also drink blue pea flower tea or peppermint tea, both of which can soothe your throat chakra. Honey is also said to be wonderful for the throat chakra, especially if you are experiencing feelings of fullness or rawness in your throat chakra.

Practical acts like singing, chanting, or speaking in a polite manner are wonderful ways to help balance your throat chakra. The more you share words of love and kindness and express yourself in a fun, loving way, the more your throat chakra will activate and balance itself. You can also compassionately assert your boundaries and lovingly express your needs, both of which will assist you in balancing your throat chakra.

If you wish to meditate on your throat chakra, lay on your back with your spine straight and your head straight forward so your throat chakra remains open and engaged. Then, begin slowly breathing in and out, allowing the energy of each passing breath to nurture your throat chakra. With each breath, feel yourself become more and more relaxed. When you start to feel at peace, visualize each passing breath drawing energy into your throat chakra. Feel your blocked throat chakra growing more empowered with each breath as you breathe life force energy into it. See the chakra glowing bright blue and rotating clockwise in a consistent, efficient manner. If your throat chakra is overactive, visualize each breath regulating it by slowing it down and releasing any excess energy with each exhale. Notice that, over time, you find yourself experiencing complete relief from your blocked or overactive chakra. When you begin to feel more balanced and at peace, allow yourself to release your meditative state and awaken back to the room around you. Repeat this meditation as often as you need to in order to fully balance your throat chakra energies.

Chapter 8: Third Eye Chakra

Your third eye chakra is the sixth of your seven physical chakras and is possibly the most popular of all of them. This chakra has numerous books written about it, including my own, titled *Third Eye Awakening*. Everyone wants to know how to tap into this chakra and the energy associated with it because it offers the opportunity to gain answers to questions that many have been asking for an eternity. Tapping into the full power of this chakra can allow you to see the unseen and access your sixth sense. It may be tempting to rush into working with the third eye chakra, but I caution you not to. Working with your third eye chakra before activating and balancing your lower five chakras can lead to an intense and overwhelming experience. If you want to experience positive, enjoyable power through this chakra, be patient, and work your way there. Rushing *will* lead to trauma and overwhelm, which may then lead to extremely stubborn blockages or overactive energies in this chakra. Be patient, then when you are ready, work with it in a meaningful way.

Third Eye Chakra Overview

Your *Ajna,* or your third eye chakra, represents your mental abilities, your psychology, and your capacity to engage in meaningful self-awareness and reflection. As well, your third eye chakra is known famously for allowing you to access extrasensory experiences. This chakra is represented by the color indigo and is often viewed as being an actual third eye that "opens" in the center of your forehead, giving you the ability to "see" into the unseen, or that which lies beyond the physical realm.

Correspondences and Connections

Your third eye chakra helps you with practical physical experiences, as well as paranormal or mystical experiences. Because of this, many things correspond with it.

If you wish to use herbs to work with your third eye chakra, reach for herbs like lemon balm, bacopa, mug wort, rosemary, star anise, or juniper. You can also use skullcap, which is well-known for supporting people with balancing their extrasensory abilities. If you have an overactive third eye chakra, skullcap is especially helpful as it will prevent unwanted nightmares, visions, and other extrasensory experiences from "taking over." Essential oils like marjoram, sage, and sandalwood are all excellent for your third eye chakra, too.

If you wish to work with crystals, use crystals like aquamarine, citrine, diamond, sugilite, smoky quartz, or amethyst. Lay one over your third eye during meditation, or, wear them as a necklace or earrings to keep them close to your third eye. You can also carry one with you, or sleep with one under your pillow or mattress if you need assistance in a more continuous way.

Lastly, your third eye chakra corresponds with your brain and your eyes. All that you see, including your conscious and subconscious thoughts, are all controlled by your third eye chakra. Your imagination and mental creativity are also controlled by your third eye, offering you the ability to visualize your desires and conceive ideas about what you wish for in life. Your unique personality, psychology, and character are also governed by your third eye chakra.

Characteristics and Energetic "Personality"

Your third eye carries with it the personality of being "all-knowing," as well as the ability to communicate with otherworldly energies and beings. All of your natural or intuitive wisdom, as well as your innate ability to "just know" things, stems from your third eye chakra, as well. Your third eye chakra invokes questions like "What am I?" "Where do I come from?" and "Why do we all exist in this Universe?". It also has the power to answer these questions, with you 'downloading' the answers from higher energies.

The third eye longs to show you what could be, aiming to bring forth visions of the things you desire in a way that allows you to manifest them in real life. Every memory you can recall, and every personal experience you have ever had relates to your third eye chakra, including the ways these experiences continue to affect you to this very day. Anytime you engage in the physical and non-physical worlds, you are engaging through your third eye chakra. It truly wants to show you how to gain the most out of everything in life, whether that be life experiences or the world around you as a whole.

Influence on Your Health

Your third eye chakra can significantly impact your mental and emotional health, and as a result, it can affect your physical health, too. For example, if your third eye chakra is imbalanced and invokes depression, you might find yourself being unable to take care of your physical self because the energy will cease to exist. When your third eye chakra is balanced, you are grounded, have a strong and healthy psyche, and enjoy a healthy emotional spectrum. You also have a strong ability to manifest your desires, as everything you want seems to just "appear" from the non-physical before your very eyes. If your third eye is imbalanced, you may have hallucinations, nightmares, vivid dreams, delusions, or you may feel entirely ungrounded from reality. In extreme cases, this may manifest as paranoia, schizophrenia, or other mental illnesses.

Lessons of the Third Eye Chakra

The third eye chakra wants to teach you about the joys of living on earth, and the value of the many things you both can and cannot see. It strives to show you the energy that exists beyond your eyes. The more you witness these energies, the more you can leverage them for your personal gain. Whether it be to manifest better or to simply experience greater gratitude for, and connection to, the world around you, the awakened third eye can teach you plenty. This chakra gives you a "connection" to the greater reality of the world around you without interfering with your ability to engage in the reality you are presently living within. When you keep this chakra balanced, you experience wonderful manifestations in life as a result.

Symptoms of a Blocked Third Eye Chakra

When your third eye chakra is blocked, your foresight is short and inadequate. You may experience headaches, migraines, blurred vision, and an inability to use your imagination or see the truth of the world around you. You may lack dreams, both in your sleep and in terms of life goals, and also lack the ability to manifest your desires into real life. Rather than tapping into your strengths, you may feel blocked from them, and it may seem like the odds are unfairly stacked against you.

Symptoms of an Overactive Third Eye Chakra

Overactive third eye chakras are easily recognizable, and they can be highly traumatic for the individual experiencing them. You might experience delusions, vivid dreams, nightmares, hallucinations, and an inability to decipher the difference between reality and imagination. Your clair senses may be overactive, as well, causing you to experience paranoia and fear of all the energies that are penetrating your field and overwhelming your system. Fear, anxiety, uncertainty, aggression, and a complete lack of touch with reality are all common in people whose third eye chakras are particularly overactive. If you do not balance your overactive third eye chakra, you might find yourself refusing to work with it again once it has been balanced because of how overwhelming the experience was. Some people will purposefully block their third eye chakra after it being overactive because of how traumatic the experience is for them. This is why it is so important to balance the first 5 chakras before attempting to work with the third eye chakra.

Routine for a Balanced Third Eye Chakra

If your third eye chakra is balanced, you can incorporate it as the sixth chakra in your full chakra healing from Chapter 10. Otherwise, you will need to engage in specific healing sessions to cure your blocked, or overactive, third eye chakra.

For your third eye chakra, eating a proper brain-healthy diet rich in Omega-3s and fatty acids is important, as this will aid your brain's natural functions. You can also avoid foods that are known for calcifying the pineal gland, as the pineal gland is the physical anchor of your third eye, and when it becomes calcified, it shrinks and is unable to work as efficiently. Eating foods high in saturated fats, sugars, or using anything that has fluoride can result in your third eye becoming calcified.

When you meditate, lay down and lay a small tumbled crystal of either amethyst or lepidolite over your third eye, both of which can help heal this chakra. Then, begin engaging in a deep, cleansing breath. As you breathe in, visualize all of your lower chakras balancing, and as you exhale, visualize them being pulled into a deeper state of alignment. When you feel relaxed enough, focus on drawing your awareness into your third eye, and visualize the chakra as it is. Notice if it's too bright or dull, and if it is moving consistently or if it is rotating too fast or too slowly. Once you know, use your breath to steady the brightness and rotation, so it moves at a consistent pace and glows a beautiful indigo color. When it feels balanced, release yourself from the meditative state and awaken to the room around you again. Repeat this meditation as often as you need to in order to balance your third eye chakra.

Chapter 9: Crown Chakra

Your crown chakra is the seventh and final chakra. This chakra houses the most pure and subtle, yet most powerful energies that you can possibly experience, as through this chakra you experience a full sense of connection to the universe and source energy. Because of how pure this chakra is, there are very few correspondences, and it provides very few lessons and experiences, yet it is an important chakra, nonetheless. This is the chakra that serves as the gateway to enlightenment.

Crown Chakra Overview

Your *Sahasrara,* or crown chakra, is the final chakra on your physical body, yet it is actually located slightly above your physical body just above the crown of your head, and directly over the top of your spine. This chakra is represented by the color violet and is often symbolized as a lotus with a thousand petals opening to receive energy from the universe. Some people view this chakra as being represented by the color white, as well, claiming the violet flame or violet light burns so bright it turns white in color.

Correspondences and Connections

Bacopa, calendula, holy basil, ginkgo, lavender, lemon balm, mugwort, peppermint, sage, rosemary, iris, violet, and lotus are all herbs that can be associated with your crown chakra. Each of these can purify your energy and help awaken you to the world around you. If you are working with essential oils or incense, reach for Palo Santo, rose, sandalwood, sage, frankincense, or cedarwood. Each of these can purify the energy in your space, making it easier for you to activate and work with your crown chakra, while facilitating a connection to the universe.

Crystals like amethyst, diamond, sapphire, rutilated quartz, ruby, scepter amethyst, and sugilite are all excellent for your crown chakra. You can wear them as necklaces or earrings, or even in barrettes or combs as hairpieces if you want to keep them close to the crown of your head. Alternatively, lay down while meditating and place one directly above your head on the surface you are laying on to receive the energy from that crystal.

Physically, your crown chakra corresponds with your hands, brain, and pituitary gland. It also helps govern your nervous system, as your nervous system controls the energy within your body, and that energy is directly associated with source energy.

Characteristics and Energetic "Personality"

Your crown chakra carries the purest energy, offering a gateway to source energy and the opportunity for you to experience enlightenment. It is said that if you awaken, balance, and master all of your chakras, the crown chakra is the last one to be mastered before you experience enlightenment. As you activate and master this chakra, you will further empower your lower chakras and enlighten them, too, as energy will be drawn down from your crown into the rest of your chakras. Soon, the boundaries between yourself and the divine vanish as you feel yourself merging into one with the divine source energies. When this has been accomplished, you have experienced total enlightenment within your crown chakra, and your entire spirit. Be aware; this takes much more time and energy than you might anticipate, as true mastery of all the chakras is a work of devotion, not just one of consistency.

Influence on Your Health

When your crown chakra is balanced, your nervous system is healthy and responds in a logical, rational, and useful manner. You experience clarity in your mind, the effortless ability to engage in physical acts of kindness, and a sense of connection in your life that is often indescribable unless you have personally experienced it. Your nervous system may be stimulated in a way that makes everything feel peaceful and reasonable, which makes navigating situations of fear and excitement much easier as you are not being overactivated in either direction. Of course, if your crown chakra is badly imbalanced, you might experience a lack of motivation, a sense of overwhelm, feelings of anxiety, or lack of energy depending on which direction the chakra has become imbalanced in.

Lessons of the Crown Chakra

The primary lesson of your crown chakra is that there is more to life than the physical world around you, and that you are more than just a physical incarnation. You are a soul having a physical experience on earth, and while you should certainly enjoy that physical experience, you should never attach yourself so greatly to it that you fail to see the bigger picture of the universe and the world around you. The relationship you share with the universe is unique to you and offers highly personal benefits. Of course, what you do and who you are in this physical form does not matter nearly as much as you might have previously thought, because at the end of the day it is all just a temporary experience. Your Truth is that you are a part of the All, and so your experience on Earth is just a summary of the choices you make during this brief version of your soul's existence.

Symptoms of a Blocked Crown Chakra

If your crown chakra is blocked, which is common before you intentionally awaken it, you will likely experience skepticism and disconnect. You might feel unsupported, as though you lack a deeper connection to anyone or anything around you, and that you are isolated or alienated from the rest of the universe. When you lack a sense of unity and closeness to everything on a deeper level, it is likely that your crown chakra is blocked. Some people might also feel a pressure or a dull headache lingering in the crown of their head, indicating the blockage. If it seems as though your lower six chakras can only experience so much before becoming "stuck", or as though no amount of effort brings them into true alignment, this also indicates a blocked crown chakra.

Symptoms of an Overactive Crown Chakra

If your crown chakra is overactive, you might find yourself ignoring human reality and believing that everyone is the cause of their own suffering, or that suffering is not real. You might lack compassion, suggesting everyone just needs to "become enlightened" because their problems are make-believe, or that they are causing their own problems. In some cases, this may be true. However, systemic racism, national poverty, and other conditions are also responsible for much of people's suffering, and these are beyond control. Dismissing people's reality in favor of "enlightenment" is a huge sign of an overactive chakra. This often happens when people first activate their chakra or when they activate it and work with it without routinely grounding themselves or working with a mentor to learn how to safely and appropriately balance their behavior. At the end of the day, you do not get to decide what does or does not constitute as suffering, or why someone else is suffering, or if those reasons are "good enough." Other's experiences are not your own, and being dismissive is not enlightenment, it's rude. If you recognize yourself behaving this way, it is a good idea to spend time balancing your crown chakra.

Routine for a Balanced Crown Chakra

If your crown chakra is already balanced, then a full chakra meditation will easily support you with maintaining that balance. Otherwise, you can lay down on the ground with a crystal over your crown chakra and begin the process of meditating to elevate the energy of this chakra. You might also prefer to sit cross legged and keep your hands on your legs, palm up, and maintain a straight spine so that your crown chakra is pointed up and away from the earth, directly toward source energy. There is no right or wrong position for this, as long as you feel open, aware, and relaxed.

Once you are in a meditative state, start visualizing the energy of your breath awakening your crown chakra. You may visualize a lotus with a thousand petals opening, or simply visualize the chakra itself as a violet spinning disc coming into balance over your crown chakra. Spend several moments breathing into your crown chakra, inviting the breath to balance your crown and relieve you of any blocked or overactive energies you might have. Once you feel balanced, allow yourself to awaken from your meditative state and come back into the room to go about your day. You can repeat this meditation as often as is necessary to keep your crown chakra balanced.

Chapter 10: Healing Your Chakras

The easiest and most time-effective way to maintain balanced, healthy chakras on a day to day basis is to have a single chakra healing meditation routine you can do each day. You can do this as you wake up while you are lying in bed, after you wake up on a meditation pillow, or at any point during the day when it feels right for you.

Before you begin meditating, make the space relaxing. Ensure you have a comfortable temperature, a proper place to sit or lie, and no distractions. You may also want to diffuse essential oil, burn incense, or light a candle to help you keep the space relaxing for your meditation.

When you are ready, close your eyes and draw your awareness to your breath. Focus on how it feels to let the breath go through you, giving yourself time to become one with your breath and body. An even pace in through your nose and out through your nose or mouth will help you begin to relax deeply, creating space for you to feel your best. When you begin to feel relaxed, you can start focusing on drawing your chakras into a state of alignment.

Start by focusing on your root chakra. Visualize it coming into its proper location, glowing bright red, and rotating clockwise. Breathe in to infuse it with positive energy, and exhale to release any unwanted energy from this chakra. Continue breathing until your root chakra feels aligned, balanced, and healed.

Next, focus on your sacral chakra. Visualize the chakra coming into alignment along your spine, glowing bright orange, and rotating clockwise. As you breathe in, visualize yourself infusing it with bright, positive energy, and as you exhale, visualize yourself releasing any unwanted energy from this chakra. Continue breathing until your sacral chakra feels aligned, balanced, and healed.

Now, focus on your solar plexus chakra. Visualize this chakra coming into alignment with your spine over your solar plexus. See it glowing bright yellow and rotating clockwise. Breathe in, visualizing your breath, infusing this chakra with positive life force energy. Exhale, visualizing any blockages or unwanted energies being released from this chakra so it can come into perfect balance. Continue breathing until you feel your solar plexus chakra is aligned, balanced, and healed.

Draw your awareness up to your heart chakra. Visualize this chakra coming into alignment along your spine, over your heart center. Notice it glowing bright green and rotating clockwise. As you inhale, visualize yourself infusing it with peaceful, positive energy. As you exhale, visualize any blockages or unwanted energy being released from this chakra. Continue breathing here until you feel your heart chakra is aligned, balanced, and healed.

Now, draw your awareness up to your throat chakra. Visualize this chakra aligning over the hollow of your throat. Notice it glowing bright blue and rotating consistently in a clockwise motion. Inhale, infusing your throat chakra with positive energy, and exhale releasing any unwanted energy from this chakra. Continue this breathing pattern until you feel your throat chakra is aligned, balanced, and healed.

Next, draw your awareness up to your third eye chakra. Visualize this chakra aligning over the center of your forehead. See it glowing bright indigo and rotating clockwise. As you breathe in, infuse positive energy into your third eye chakra, and as you exhale, release any unwanted energy from it. Continue breathing until you feel your third eye chakra is aligned, balanced, and healed.

Finally, focus on your crown chakra. Visualize this chakra aligning over your crown, glowing violet, and rotating clockwise. As you inhale, infuse positive energy into your crown chakra, and as you exhale, release any unwanted energy from it. Continue breathing until you feel your crown chakra is aligned, balanced, and healed.

When you are done, take several breaths to allow yourself to enjoy the feeling of having balanced chakras. As you begin to feel more relaxed here, awaken from your meditation and move your awareness back into the room around you. Allow yourself to spend a few minutes reflecting and enjoying this positive experience either by soaking it in or journaling about it before you go about your daily routine. If you are going to be wearing or carrying any crystals or other chakra tools with you throughout the day, now would be the time to put them on, as you are balanced and ready to set your daily intentions.

Conclusion

Congratulations on completing this book on *Chakras!*

This book was designed to help you create a deeper sense of connection to yourself and your chakras. The more you work with your chakras, the more you will find yourself enjoying a deeper relationship with yourself and a greater understanding of the very essence of your life. All of your experiences and the energy you enjoy from life will be far greater if you awaken your chakras, and work with them regularly.

I hope that after reading this book, you feel more connected to yourself, the universe, and the world around you. I hope you now also feel confident in your abilities to balance and maintain the health of your chakras.

After reading this book, I encourage you to start balancing your chakras from the root chakra, up. Give yourself the time and space you need to master each chakra, so that you can create a solid foundation for each following chakra that you work with. As you do this, you will find yourself enjoying a stronger level of connection to yourself, your energy, and the world and universe around you.

Once again, I'd like to thank you for taking the time to read this book. I hope you found it to be helpful!

www.ingramcontent.com/pod-product-compliance
Lightning Source LLC
Chambersburg PA
CBHW071507030726
47593CB00003B/1195